Bondage
for beginners

THIS IS A CARLTON BOOK

Text, illustrations and design copyright © Carlton Books Limited 2009

This edition published by
Carlton Books Limited
20 Mortimer Street
London W1T 3JW

10 9 8 7 6 5 4 3 2 1

ISBN 978 1 84732 453 5

Printed and bound in China

Senior Executive Editor: Lisa Dyer
Managing Art Director: Lucy Coley
Copy editor: Nicky Gyopari
Designer: Anna Pow
Production: Kate Pimm

Bondage

for beginners

Tie-me-up
tricks
and knots

Lisa Sweet

CARLTON
BOOKS

Contents

Introduction   6

1: Lesson Plans   10

2: Tools of the Trade   22

3: Why Knot?   48

4: Pleasure Bound   78

Bondage Directory   114

Introduction

• •

You don't have to study specialized lingo, invest in a treasure chest of ropes, chains and cuffs, or even get off on pain (dishing or receiving it) to get pleasure from the idea of slipping some bondage into your bedroom romps. In fact, you don't even have to call it bondage.

Erotic bondage is so much more than tying up someone you love and tantalizingly torturing them. What it's really about is playing around with control in your love play – one of you gets to act helpless, the other gets to have their deliriously dastardly way. Dabbling in these sorts of power games can add a kick to your carnal connections – especially when you've been doing the same-old with each other for a while and crave something with a bit more spice than organizing yourselves into a new pretzel position. The knowledge that you can do or have done what you will (within reason!) for your mutual moaning pleasure is mind-blowing. Plus the tight constriction that comes with being restrained can be a sensory trip in itself, pumping up adrenalin and leading to more intense, more blissful – and simply more – orgasms.

The by-the-way message here is that you *are* a couple. Getting friskier and riskier between the sheets requires a certain amount of trust, intimacy and comfort. You can't get bonded with restraints until you've bonded with your hearts (the kinky set credo is "Safe, Sane and Consensual"). But once you are ready to raunch up your regular repertoire, getting bold with bondage can actually help tighten your connection in and out of the bedroom. Knowing that you can trust each other enough to respect each

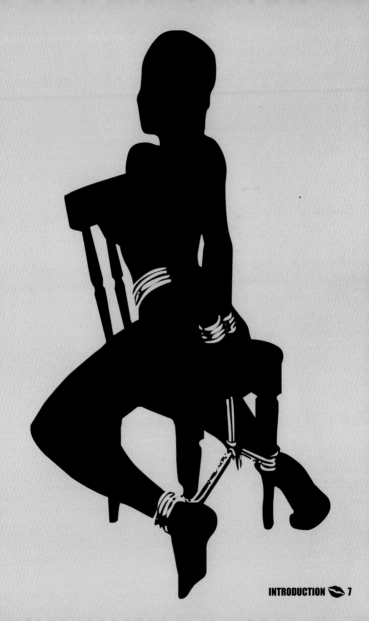

other's emotional and sexual needs, curiosity and boundaries can be a pretty potent force in deepening love and affection.

So why do people get tied up with bondage in their sex play? There's no one reason. Some love the idea of giving up all of the control and being completely ravished by their partner in passion. There's nothing more exciting than having someone under your rule – unless it's being at their mercy. Others find the actual sensation of the restraints deliciously divine. For others, it's the idea of taking an erotic walk on the wild side that makes their toes curl. Sometimes, it's just another fun game to play. And some people don't know why they do it – it just feels oh!-so-good.

You may make bondage a part of your everyday sex life or it could be something you indulge in occasionally, like a double-scoop hot fudge ice-cream sundae or reading your lover's emails.

Of course, there's a wider playing field in bondage than tying wrists to the bedposts. In general there are three types of bondage: **restrain** bondage, where the goal is to restrict someone's range of motion; **stimulation** bondage where, rather than keep them in check, the ropes or ties are there to make them writhe by rubbing against sensitive bits of the body; and **suspension** bondage – which is pretty much how it sounds – a person is bound from an overhead fixture using a harness or sling that will dangle their arms, legs or entire body off of the floor, adding a suspenseful edge of tension to the proceedings.

By the end of this book, you will know how to tie a body harness, safely put on a gag, secure someone to a table or a chair or tie their hands behind their back or above their head. And you will do it all safely and with style.

Chapter One
Lesson Plans

Rope has a long and knotted history – it has been used as everything from a toy, clothing accessory and decoration to a tool, weapon and torture device. So it's not surprising that the practice of sexual bondage has been kicking around for a while. It's mentioned in the *Kama Sutra* and the writings of the Marquis de Sade, as well as Anne Rice's *Sleeping Beauty* novels (where she uses the pen name A N Roquelaure). It received a passing glance in the sexual advice bible *The Joy of Sex* and was given action in mainstream movies like *Tie Me Up, Tie Me Down*, *Pulp Fiction* and *Black Snake Moan*, to name just a few. Madonna's 1992 coffee table book, *Sex*, which included photographs of bound nudes, did its bit to improve public awareness and acceptance of bondage. By the 1990s, bondage had gone mainstream and could be found on prime-time hit television series such as *Buffy the Vampire Slayer*, where bondage gear such as handcuffs and collars and concepts such as the "safe word" were included as a matter of course. And today, is there a designer left who hasn't used bondage elements?

Eastern & Western Techniques

These days, there are two main modes of erotic bondage. From the Asian shores comes the highly ritualized bondage known as *Kinbaku* in Japan and *Shibari* in the West. One of the most imaginative of all bondage styles (and arguably the most beautiful), it developed from the Japanese military restraint technique of *Hojojutsu*. The bondage patterns still echo the martial art with a decidedly steamy slant and are a common sight in Japanese pornography and manga.

One of the main ways in which Shibari differs from Western bondage is that instead of knotting and wrapping the ropes to restrain and immobilize, the focus is on creating patterns. Putting knots on a person was regarded as extremely disgraceful, something some would regard as worse than death (although these days, most dabblers in Shibari will add a few knots just to finish things off). Instead, wrappings were developed that were thoughtfully designed and executed with beauty, functionality and safety in mind, to stimulate erotic pressure points such as the genitals, breasts and other hot zones. Think of it as origami, except that you're naked and folding rope instead of paper.

In contrast, in Western bondage, the emphasis is on the knot. Much of this style comes from photographer Irving Claw and artist John Willie. In their images, limbs are usually tied together (wrists, elbows, ankles, knees) and there is very little use of elaborate harnesses or instruments – and even less possibility of sex, considering the way the bodies have been bound!

Instead, the erotic element comes from the predicament – such as being tied to the railroad tracks, dragged behind a horse or tied to a log at a sawmill. A damsel in distress is almost always involved.

It is probable that the uniquely human pursuit of bondage as a strictly-for-pleasure erotic endeavour actually has its roots in normal biological urges. Just watch any mammal getting it on – the male will seize the neck of the female in his teeth during mating to restrain her.

But whatever the origin, what is clear is that rather than weird and kinky, this form of sexual power play is enduringly – and endearingly – popular. Studies by sexual-desire guru Nancy Friday has found that the fantasy of being bound during intercourse is second in frequency only to the basic fantasy of getting it on with a hot babe for men, while women tend to get a warm and fuzzy feeling over the thought of being tied up and helpless to protest being ravished by some mysterious handsome dude.

Bondage is clearly unbound.

SAFETY NOTE

Some of the text in this book covers risky behaviour. This may not be interpreted as expert advice. In the event of an emergency or medical issue, always consult a doctor or healthcare professional. Whenever precautions and general first aid are mentioned and described in these articles, please be aware that every individual situation is different, that the information provided is of a general nature, and that all erotic power exchange play is always and only the responsibility of the partners involved.

Play Safe

Before busting out the ball gag, get some basic safety precautions under your belt.

1 Choose a safe word. This is a pre-agreed word or phrase that stops or slows down the amorous action when spoken by either partner. The basic concept is to allow either player to shout out things like "Stop, oh no, don't, you brute! Anything but that!" but knowing that they don't really want to stop the passionate proceedings.

Common safe words are "red" for stop and "yellow" for slow down, but the word can be anything you both agree on. Most people prefer something that wouldn't normally slip out (such as "No!", "Stop!", "I love you!", "Brangelina!"). Try not to make it something terribly long or hard to remember. "A tooter who tooted the flute, tried to tutor two tooters to toot" doesn't exactly trip off the tongue. Also, try to refrain from creating complicated systems. Using "green" for "great, get going with more of that" is fine; but using "blue" for "bring in the Berkley Horse" and "violet" for "tweezer clamps" is bound to confuse things.

If you're using a gag, make your "safe word" a "safe signal". Have the person hold something in their hand – if they drop it it's time to stop. Or, if their hands or fingers are not tied up, these can be raised to put a halt to your hoopla.

2 The one tie that you should never bind is one that causes any pressure at all around the neck. Nothing acts likes a cold shower on your love play like accidentally cutting off their air supply or breaking their windpipe. Also take care with gags if your lover is asthmatic, is prone

to TMJ (Temporomandibular Disorder), has severe allergies, congestion, or any breathing problem (never stopping for breath when they talk is actually an argument for using a gag).

3 One is the loneliest number – especially in bondage. Though it is a hot fantasy to tie someone up in some precarious position (possibly with vibrators or other devices buzzing away) and then leave him or her to stew, in reality you must consider: What if the house is burgled? The room catches fire? There's an earthquake? Your mother arrives for an unexpected visit? They have to go to the toilet? The rule of thumb is to stay as close to your bound partner as you would to a baby left in your care so you can quickly release them.

4 Be prepared to cut your way out of any emergency with these two tools:

- Safety shears: These are a must if you are using rope, fabric, or leather restraints. Don't use regular scissors – or even worse, a knife – for this. If you need to break out the slashing material quickly, the chances are you'll cut your lover with those sharp points and edges. Safety shears cost little and can cut through almost any material, including sheet metal (available from most chemists).

- Bolt Cutters: Handy for cutting jammed locks, padlocks when the keys are lost and chains if necessary, as well as breaking into your local bank's vault.

What constitutes a bondage emergency? Start cutting any time your partner:

- loses consciousness
- has a freak-out panic attack
- experiences sudden, severe pain as a result of the bondage (this may mean a compressed nerve).

Don't hesitate – even if it's your most expensive locks or leather cuffs. You can always replace your equipment, but not necessarily your partner. Stay loose and easy – if you can't fit a finger between the restraint and the bound person's skin, it's too tight. Hands or other bound areas turning purple, getting pins and needles or feeling cold are also good cut-it-now indicators.

5 You don't have to be uncomfortable – unless you want to be. Certain positions are more relaxing than others. Standing spread-eagled looks great but it can rapidly become tiring. Arms over the head are another sexy pose, but lead to shoulder strain when held too long. Some of the more comfortable bondage positions include lying down on a bed, tied seated in a chair, or over the arm of a couch.

6 Hold off on suspension poses until you have learned how, hands-on, from someone who really knows what they are doing. This sort of activity requires skill and practice.

Two of the Worst Bondage Materials

1 Any cloths like scarves, bandanas or handkerchiefs tend to tighten under tension; sometimes they get so tight they have to be cut off. Save these for blindfolds and instead invest in purpose-bought cuffs or metal connectors called "panic snaps", which allow you to disconnect bonds that have weight on them.

2 Handcuffs are sexy, but they can also be a pain. Cheap cuffs are liable to break while being worn – then you have to file or cut them off. Invest in a good pair with a double lock that will hold up under pressure. Or use Velcro or press-stud (snap) quick-remove cuffs.

Become an Escape Artist

You'll be able to get yourself out of any tight situation in moments once you master these three simple tricks.

• Get your body into the groove. Keep your wrists, legs, arms or ankles apart as much as you can while being tied up. Take a deep breath to inflate your chest when the binds go around so that you can breathe easily once bound. This will make things feel nice and snug but still give you breathing and wriggle room if you have to slip out of the knots.

• As a beginner, use thick ropes, especially if you are binding yourself. Thicker rope is more difficult to work with and therefore you can't tie extremely tight knots. They are easier to untie than something very thin such as tights (pantyhose) or silk scarves.

• Free your hands first. They will help you get out of the rest of the knots you are tied up in.

Chapter Two
Tools of the Trade

You may be turned on by the idea of bondage but don't really want to make a huge investment in equipment, or even put in the study time earning your scout badge for knot tying. So don't. There's no power rule that says that you have to get all gussied up like the Gimp in *Pulp Fiction* or transform your spare room into a dungeon. Fact is, you don't need any special equipment at all – or even a rope for that matter. You can use a necktie, a scarf, a hair tie… or just your voice.

But you still need to nurture some type-A personality tendencies and get organized. Just like you can't make an omelette without breaking some eggs, you can't indulge in even the minimum of bondage play without planning ahead. Imagine – you decide to tie up your lover and then spend twenty minutes looking for something to secure them. Or you do find a belt and then, because you don't really know how to bind properly, you wrap it around their ankles so now their legs are tightly tied together, making it impossible for you to get in and play with their equipment. On the following pages are four basic steps to get you started on your power play without losing control.

STEP ONE *Top or Bottom?*

Decide who is going to be the "top" (the one dishing it out) and who is going to be the "bottom" (the one on the receiving end). You may find you prefer doing the tormenting to being tormented. Or you may have a bit of both the pushover and the persecutor in you. Fine and dandy. In every relationship, the power dynamic is constantly shifting so why should it be any different in your kinky games?

To figure out which one best suits you, take out your pencils and get ready for a pop quiz. No cheating.

Question 1

If you're in a restaurant with your lover, you:
A Sometimes order for them
B Don't throw a hissy fit if they order for you
C Don't mind who puts in the order as long as you get what you want

Question 2

When you have sex, who usually makes the first move?
A Me
B My lover
C It's mostly 50:50

Question 3

When you're in bed together, how do you normally lie?
A My partner cuddles me from behind
B I lie with my head on their chest or cuddle them from behind
C We lie close together with our arms around each other

Question 4

How do you hold hands?
A My partner's hand is tucked into mine
B My hand is tucked into my partner's
C Our fingers are linked together

If you answered mostly **A**s: You are so a "top"
If you answered mostly **B**s: Stick to being a "bottom"
If you answered mostly **C**s or a mix of **A**s, **B**s and **C**s:
You're a switch hitter and can take as good as you get, so take
turns with both roles (arm wrestle to decide, if you must).

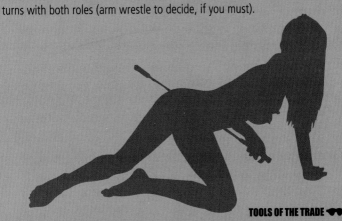

STEP TWO *Set Your Scene*

The "bottom" could just be bent over a table or bed or hitched up to a staircase railing or towel holder but where's the fun in that? There are so many easy ways to convert your boudoir into a designer-worthy dungeon for the price of a latte.

If you didn't inherit a headboard from your Great Aunt Gertrude, then get some standard-issue doorknobs or drawer pulls and eyebolts and screw them in at strategic locations. You could even put them on the sides of the bed and the bottom if you want a variety of positions in the night. It's practical, cheap, and you can move them around if you've chosen bad spots. The alternative is bondage bedwear, but it's such a hassle and expensive, and it may feel a bit too hardcore for your purposes.

If home improvement isn't your thing or drill holes aren't allowed in your lease, skip the trip to the DIY shop and order up a catalogue from your local sex shop instead. Good online sources (read: brown paper delivery) for fun bondage gear are www.temptationsdirect.co.uk, www.lovehoney. co.uk and www.annsummers.com. Get a set of portable door-jam cuffs for stand-up-and-deliver power play (they use Velcro to easily attach to any door) and bed restraints to pin bottoms down and render them helpless in moments without a single nail being hammered (they slip over any size of mattress and can be quickly unattached or hidden away under the bed).

STEP THREE *Get Some Rope*

While you can technically tie someone up with anything you can get your hands on – boating line, yarn, electrical cords, pantyhose, belts and even neck ties, eventually even the most occasional bondage dipper turns to rope. Nothing matches it for simplicity, efficiency, versatility and availability – and it feels good against the skin and practically screams: "Tie me up and ravage me!"

Rope has its downside – it's fairly easy to pull a Houdini, it can be difficult to tie properly without cutting off circulation, and it can cause nasty rope burns if the material is too rough (although that last one might be a reason to use rope for some!).

That said, rope is inexpensive and easy to get a hold of. You only need to learn a couple of knots to get started (see pages 50–53). And it's a common enough household item that your mother will never suspect its double-duty purpose if she goes snooping in your bedroom.

While most common household rope is just fine, it isn't as simple as snagging 30 m (100 ft) of clothesline at the hardware store and putting a bow on it. There's more to bondage rope than meets the eye – from choosing material to size and style preferences.

Material

- **Synthetic fibres** – usually nylon, polyester, or polypropylene ("poly")
  – are best for beginners. They're easy to find (any DIY shop worth
  its moniker will have a few reels in stock in different diameters in
  accessory-matching black, red, yellow and blue). Another choice is
  rayon (though it tends to be more expensive and is found mainly in
  boat supply stores). The strands that synthetic ropes are made of tend
  to feel slippery and look glossy, making for a soft smooth ride (nylon
  could easily double for cotton) and they're waterproof, so you can use
  them anywhere. Synthetics are also hardwearing and need minimal
  preparation (see Wash and Dry, page 33) before using them. The flip
  side, however, is that they don't hold a knot as well as other materials
  (but then, that might be a boon for a nervous newbie).

- **Natural fibres** such as hemp, cotton and sometimes jute or sisal tend
  to be stiffer, rougher and scratchier than the synthetics and may even
  leave splinters. Knots are hard to untie in cotton rope and it does not
  wear well. Hemp will become softer after being washed several times
  but it tightens when wet and is not good for suspension because it will
  rot. However, these fibres will hold knots better. This doesn't make much
  difference for most bondage play, but if you want to get into Japanese
  bondage (see pages 12–13, 53 and 104–6) then you'll want to invest in
  authentic hemp.

Tie Breakers

Match the material to your mood.

- If you want to get a little comfort and joy, choose the softer, looser nylon, "poly" or cotton ropes.

- If you want get all tied up with no place to go, get tightly tied with natural fibres.

- If you're up for being treated like a FedEx package, you'll prefer the rough handling that comes with hemp, jute and sisal.

- If you want to be a catwalk model and have the right look, natural fibres will leave telltale marks on the skin.

- If you're worried about breaking out in a rash or having a sneezing attack, stay away from natural fibres, which can cause an allergy moment.

- If you want to break the ties that bind, cotton makes even weaklings feel like the Incredible Hulk.

- If you're a beginner and don't have time to comparison shop, stick with the easy-to-work-with synthetics.

Size

Beginners should start with thicker rope but not too thick. To hold knots
well and be practical, rope should be smaller than 25 mm (1 in) thick. The
best diameters run between 5 mm and 13 mm (¹/₅ in and ½ in). Broadly
speaking, thinner rope is easier to tie, but "bites" the skin more. Thicker
rope feels gentler but is harder to tie good knots in. Usually, it's a case
of like for like – larger bottoms enjoy the feel of thick rope that is 10 mm
(³/₈ in) or more and smaller bottoms prefer thinner rope that is 6 mm (¼ in)
or less.

On the whole, it's better to have too much rope for a given tie than not
enough, but if the rope is too long or too short, tying the knots will be
difficult and create unsexy "tails" at the end. For a full basic bondage set,
figure on around 80 m (265 ft) of rope cut up as follows, plus 4 m (13 ft)
for mistakes:

1 x 14 m (49 ft): body harnesses for most average-size people
4 x 9 m (30 ft): chest harnesses, crotch ropes, body harnesses
    on smaller people
3 x 5 m (16 ft): ties on knees, ankles, or elbows; wrist ties where
        you want some rope left over for tying to something, for making
        rope "cuffs" for each wrist or ankle
2 x 3 m (10 ft): basic wrist or ankle ties
4 x 2 m (7 ft): for securing leather cuffs to furniture or hooks.

The ropes can be of different colours to show lengths.
Use an old magician's trick and mark the centre to make
it easier for quick and even folding.

Style

The best bondage rope comes in two basic forms: twisted or braided. If you're using synthetic rope, braided is the only way to go. It may be hollow, solid or have a core. These are not personality judgements for how they are used; rather, hollow is just that – it has no centre but it's still a favourite because it has a wicked snake-like appearance and a smooth sensation. Solid is pure braid and used for its thickness while core is just what it sounds like – a braided sheath over a fibre core for extra strength (the materials on the cover and the core can be different). There is a good stepsister to this trio: braid on braid, which is very strong but also very pricey.

Twisted rope is soft and good-looking, like a socialite. The fibres are wound into three thick strands that are then turned in the same direction. These coils can leave an impression on the skin which can last anything from a few minutes to several hours (so have a cover-up handy just in case).

Wash and Dry

- Once you have cut your rope to the desired length, seal the ends to stop them from fraying. You can use a few tight wraps of duct or electrical tape or, if its synthetic rope, melt them by holding the section you want to cut over a flame and then cutting after you melt (this helps avoid big, rough globs of melted rope at the ends).

- Almost all good bondage rope (except hemp) can be washed in the washing machine. Just put it in a pillowcase tied in a knot and then wash it on the warm cycle. Put your rope in the dryer without heat (to avoid shrinkage) or hang it up to dry.

- Try not to store your rope using the "big tangle in the bottom of the closet" method. Instead, coil up your rope by grabbing the middle of the rope and doubling it. Hold one end in your hand and use the other hand to wrap the doubled rope around from your hand to elbow. Then wrap the last loop around the bundle and knot it with a half-knot. It's worth the effort to be a neat bondage freak because you won't end up having to deal with unexpected knots and twists in your rope mid-play. Plus, bending instead of coiling can weaken the rope's fibre strength.

- Check for signs of wear or discolouration (which signals chemical damage) and discard any suspicious-looking rope that looks like it will not bear weight, even if you don't use it for suspension.

Strung Out

If you're a beginner intimidated by rope or don't have any in the house, scarves may seem like a great stepping-stone. But this is not a good idea. DO NOT tie up your partner with scarves – they're practically impossible to loosen once knotted (especially if they're silk) and can cut off circulation. If you absolutely must, leave 15 cm (6 in) tails when knotting off and release will be easier. And keep scissors handy (Hermès scarf owners, take note).

Much safer, though, is to tear an old bedsheet into long strips that are 15 cm (6 in) wide. They're comfortable, knot well and untie easily. A knotted sheet strip is also strong enough to be used for standing positions. Fold the strip, tie a half-knot in it, set it over the door and shut it securely, with the knot on the other side of the door. Tie other strips through the resulting loop that hangs down from the door.

Now get slammin'.

STEP FOUR *Choosing Extras*

Do you want your bondage play to be low- or high-bondage maintenance? If you're just starting out or are extra-sensitive, then all you really need is a necktie, a long sock, a leather belt, a scarf, a cotton handkerchief or scrunchie for some down-and-dirty, off-the-cuff B&B (Bondage and Blindfold) and Bob's your uncle – or, at least, you'll soon be shouting uncle. Or just shouting.

Even if you decide to play hardball, you don't need to clean out your local sex shop of its bondage toys. Your home is chock-a-block with loads of things that can sub as power tools. Forks, pastry brushes (especially the silicone kinds), belts, ties, scarves, sandpaper, exfoliating gloves, ice cubes and hair ties are just a few of the everyday items that can pull double duty. Two items to avoid: zip-ties (they may seem like a good idea as an unbreakable tie, but they tend to cut into flesh and are especially bad when used to bind a limb to something else) and electrical cords (they don't hold knots well, making the result less than electric).

Load what you plan to use on a carrying tray so everything you need is close to hand. And the "top" should blindfold the "bottom" before bringing over the tray – half the tantalizing titillation is in not knowing what is going to happen next.

Must-Have Items for Bondage Beginners

Blindfolds
These come in every material imaginable from satin to leather to fleece-lined. They're usually thicker than the kind used for sleeping to prevent the "bottom" from peeking at the proceedings. Anticipation is everything.

Cuffs
Handcuffs are the classic form of restraint, which makes them most popular for novices. Plus they're cheap. But there's a lot that can go wrong with handcuffs. Too much. You can lose the key, and even if you don't lose the key, the lock often gets jammed (especially with novelty items like furry cuffs). Cuffs are uncomfortable; they can really dig into skin and they may cause nerve damage. To avoid disaster and embarrassing trips to the hospital, invest in the fancier metal handcuffs, which have thin keys with pin-point tops to prevent jams and overtightening.

Better yet, go soft. Nylon cuffs wrap around the wrists or ankles and fasten with a buckle or Velcro, making them a cinch to get out of; they're wide and padded so they don't pinch wrists or ankles, or cut off blood circulation. So they're a tad more expensive than the metal and furry cuffs, but aren't you worth it?

Silk Binding Sash
You don't need to know how to do any kind of intricate binding with these. A simple bow is easy to get out of and looks beautiful.

Bondage Sheets

You won't get this mattress sheet as a wedding present! It comes with four nylon cuffs with Velcro for wrists and ankles and makes getting in and out of the control game a snap — perfect for putting a restraining order on your lovemaking without much fuss.

Full Set

Many sex shops (see page 26) sell bondage beginner kits, which include some combo of a blindfold, cuffs, vibrator, whip or paddle and clamps. Great if you prefer one-stop shopping.

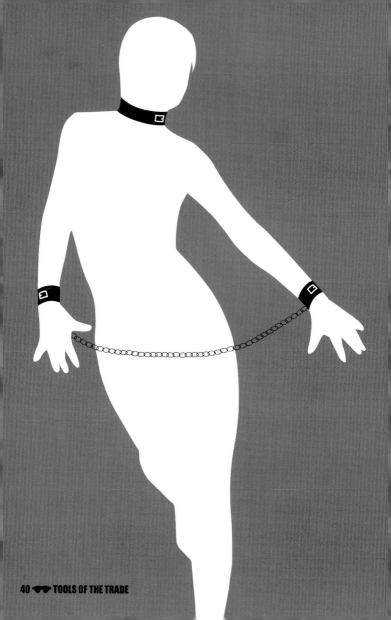

For Advanced Prisoners of Love

Collar

Choose either the real doggie thing, one specially made out of leather or even a thin locking chain. Some players use collars as an accessory; others find wearing one is an instant way to signify that play is about to start (your bondage scene begins when the collar is on and ends when it's off). Some come with rings for attaching leads (leashes) or restraints, though any neck play can cause suffocation so you're probably better off just using it as an accessory. Always make sure that you can fit a few fingers between the choker/collar and the wearer's skin. Also be sure that there isn't too much pulling or stress on the neck.

Gag

You can use anything that goes over the mouth to give your play a quick damsel- (or lad-) in-distress makeover. Because covering the mouth can give a nasty bout of asphyxia (which seems to be a running theme with these props), it does make sense to use one made for the purpose (although medical cloth can do in a pinch). The most popular is the ball gag, which is usually a small ball – 5 cm (2 in) is the largest even the biggest mouths can handle – made of rubber or silicone that is placed in the mouth behind the teeth, with straps going around the head to secure it in place. The purpose isn't to drown out cries, but rather to make your partner sound exactly as helpless as they are.

Leather Cuffs

These bad boys have a sexy look and usually fasten with buckles. They're also on the wide side and can be a bit too weighty. If leather isn't your thing or you're a vegan, there are leather-like cuffs as well, continuing the artificial theme with a faux-fur lining.

Hood

There are a few different types but the safest (because it doesn't block breathing, leaving you with a snooded corpse) is known as the ponygirl hood. Basically, it covers the wearer's entire head and neck with a large opening in front in a way that brings to mind a nun's habit (which is an entirely different type of fantasy). These hoods may have a small opening at the top, so if the wearer has long hair, it can be tightly gathered, threaded through and left hanging down the back of the head as a ponytail and used for hair bondage (see page 98).

Wartenberg Wheel

Originally developed by neurologists to test dermal nerve response, savvy bondage users like the way they can run the steely, bright 22-point wheel over legs, breasts, backs, genitals… wherever they want to create a shiver.

Spreader Bar

Think cop in a closet – these bars are designed to keep feet or hands spread.

Cock Rings

These come in everything from cold hard metal to flesh-like silicone with or without a lead (leash) – putting an entirely new meaning on walking the dog. The main purpose is to delay his booty boogie until his master tells him he can come to the party.

TOOLS OF THE TRADE 💭 43

Striker

Although S&M and bondage go together like fish and chips (or peanut butter and jelly if you're North American), power play tends to be more about playing with sensation than inflicting pain. So choose your material carefully, depending on how much pain you want to gain.

- **Whips:** Anything made of soft materials like cotton rope that has been frayed, the bristles on a paintbrush, horsehair and rubber duster whips will all let you play with power, but no pain. Whips made of leather deliver sting. The general rule of thumb is the heavier the material it's made from, the stingier the feeling. Also, if the tips have a rounded edge to them, they'll be less painful than a whip that has tips cut at an angle or metal at its end.

- **Paddles:** Use only if you're serious about delivering pain – these can pack a punch because they're usually wide and flat. Again, the level of the ouch depends on the material – hard things like wood will serve up a good smack while those made from fabric will give a softer blow.

- **Slappers:** Think paddles on a detox diet. The kicker is the two (usually leather) flaps sewn together on one side, which makes its bark worse than its actual bite.

- **Riding crops:** Use these 60 cm (2 ft) rods to look menacing and stress dominance without actually inflicting any pain.

- **Canes:** These are what you graduate up to when a riding crop just doesn't do it for you any more. Made of thin wood, nylon, fibreglass, bamboo or leather, they really, really sting under any strike (use them once and next time you'll feel the pain just looking at them).

Straightjackets

These are a quick and easy way to completely immobilize someone. But they are not comfortable (hence the name), so only use when you are doing a short scene.

Hanging Chair

These come in different forms, such as porch swings, hanging macramé chairs, net chairs and basket chairs. Read the instructions about how to put the bolts into the ceiling unless you want to end up with a collapsed chair with your lover inside. You can buy bolts separately from the chairs. To make your plaything look part of the décor when not in use, hang a plant, mobile or chimes from the hook.

Cinch It Up

Historically, corsets – like bras – were closely linked with keeping women "in their proper place". Certain medieval designs were literally torture devices made from steel. Later, actual whalebones were used, which were extremely strong and inflexible (and often resulted in broken ribs). The Victorians showed their repressed paranoid roots in complicated corset knots that meant corsets doubled up as chastity belts. They even invented crotchless "pettipants" so that women could use the toilet without removing their corsets.

Once fantastic elastics came on the scene, girdles replaced corsets and the device went underground (literally into the dungeons) as bondage wear. These corsets come in everything from leather to PVC and are made from bendable spring or spiral binds that bend to fit the curves of the body, comfortably restricting and reducing the waist by 5–10 cm (2–4 in). Now that's a much more fun way to go for the burn!

Chapter Three

Why Knot?

Bondage is about bodies — not the knots. The rope — or however you're tying things on — is just the hardware. Anything you can do with your arms or hands, you can do with a rope. So use it to hold your partner tight or loose, to grab a wrist or an ankle or to put those legs right where you want them.

And don't get yourself tied up in knots about how you work your restraints. The fact is, there is no single "right way" to tie someone up. There are thousands. Most come from sailors who didn't have much else to do when they were stuck for years on end in the middle of the ocean. Luckily, landlubbers really need to know only a few nuts and bolts to get them in (and out) of any steamy bondage scenario. The rest is gravy — very saucy gravy, but gravy all the same.

Teaching the Ropes

Your essential all-purpose moves to becoming a bondage master. Look on www.iwillknot.com for step-by-step instructions for most common knots. Before you start, practise these two techniques until you can do them in your sleep:

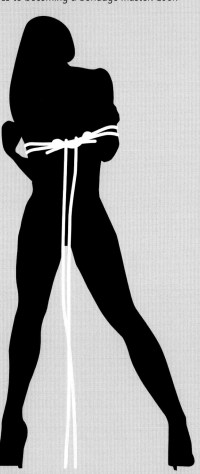

1 Bight: Essentially an open loop – fold the rope in half at the middle.

2 Lark's Head: Pass the loose tails of the rope through the bight. To use it on an object (any part of the body, on furniture or a handle), wrap the rope around the object with the loop in front, and slip the tail ends through the loop from the opposite side.

Although not knots, the bight and Lark's Head will form the base of most bindings.

Square or Reef Knot

This is the most commonly used knot, useful for tying packages, finishing off surgery, and your partner.

How To Do It: If you can tie your shoes, you can make a Square knot. It's just like the first part of tying your shoes, and for the second part you repeat the first half in the opposite direction. Remember "right over left, left over right, makes a Square knot nice and tight!" Tighten by pulling the loose ends.

Don't Come Untied: If you tie right over left, right over left, you will end up with two twisted ropes known as granny knot, which isn't really much of a knot since it slips until it unties itself.

Half Hitch

Slightly more fiddly, this tie is best used for tying a rope to a piece of furniture such as a bedpost. It shouldn't be used on any part of the body, or for suspension.

How To Do It: Hook the rope around what you're going to bind and bring the short end under the long end, then over the top of the long end and through the space between the object and the rope. Pull tight to secure. Do two more times to create a "hitch and a half".

Don't Come Untied: It's possible for a Half Hitch to slip, but if you do three in a row, it's virtually impossible to come apart.

That's it. You are done. You now have all of the information you need to restrain your lover in pretty much any configuration your twisted little heart desires.

Shibari Ties

If you lean more towards the East in your bondage know-how, the fundamentals of Shibari are slightly different but still fairly simple:

1 **Folding or Bight:** You still need the bight (see page 50) – in fact, almost all Japanese rope bondage is based on this fold.

2 **Banding:** Continue to fold and refold the bight into bands or layers. The idea is that the more bands you have, the quicker you use up the rope when wrapping. Beginners should stick with one or two bands; experts can work with as much as they can handle without coming undone.

3 **Layering:** Take several different pieces of rope or techniques and layer them on top of each other for a combo meal. For example, make a chest harness (see Karada, pages 72–73) , then taking another rope, use one of the ends to tie to the chest harness and tie the other end to a beam.

Beyond Basic Knots

Bondage knots are a bit like eating chips. No one can ever stop at one. So once you have the basics, start practising the following ties. Slightly more complicated, they will let you weave a bit more style into your loop-de-loops.

Bar Wrap

A thrifty, elegant way to use up extra rope, bar none. Basically, you take the tails of rope and wrap them around a band of rope nice and tight so that you end up making a handle that you can actually grab and lift with.

How To Do It: Loop the rope around the object you're tying to. Hold an end in each hand. Cross the end in your right hand over the end in your left, forming an X with your hands and holding the pieces at the top of the X. Wrap the end in your right hand around the object again in the same direction as before, leaving the wrap loose. When you bring it back around to the front, poke the end under the piece of rope that you've just wrapped around.

Don't Come Untied: If you don't keep working your ends in the same direction, you will end up with a knotted mess.

French Bowline Knot

A good knot for binding wrists and ankles
because it won't accidentally tighten and cut
off circulation. You can prepare them in advance as cuffs.

How To Do It: Lay the rope straight and then make a small loop in it,
leaving a long tail. Coil the long end around the limb three or four times,
each time going through the small loop. On the last trip through the loop,
wrap the long end under the short end and back through the small loop
in the opposite direction.

Don't Come Untied: Don't tighten as you coil – you don't want it to
be too loose or too tight – and then slide and pull the loops until they fit
snugly and neatly.

Buntline Hitch

A fast way to tie a rope to a fixed object such as a suspension bar or
a bedpost, but not to a person because the loop tightens under tension
and could restrict circulation.

How To Do It: Loop the rope around the object (once or more). Pass the
short end over the main rope segment to make a figure-of-eight, then pass
it under and over the long end in a figure-of-eight in the opposite direction.
Pull to tighten.

Don't Become Undone: Pull too soon and everything will slip.

The Prusik

This is the knot you should use if you want to tighten the rope after binding, for instance, for having your sub (submissive) very tense after spread-eagling her. When not under tension, sliding the knot along the rope is easy. When tightened by the tension, it locks.

How To Do It:

1 Make a Lark's Head (see page 50) and slip it over your partner's hand or foot so that it is around their wrist or ankle. Take the long tails and move them in the opposite direction so the loop is open and slack. The loop should be on the outside, away from the body, and the long tails on the inside, towards the body.

2 Reach through the loop and pull the long ends of the rope through. Pull on the loop again, to get some more slack, and wrap the loop around again. You may have to keep creating more slack to help the ropes move around the wrist or ankle.

3 Reach through the loop again, and pull the long ends through. Pull on the long ends, helping the ropes move around the wrist or ankle, until the wraps are comfortably snug, but not tight. Take one of the long ends and pass it under three of the wraps, starting at the outside and pulling it out the middle. Pull the end taut.

4 Take the other long end and pass it under three of the wraps, starting at the outside and pulling it out the middle. Pull the end taut. Repeat, taking one of the long ends and passing it under three of the wraps, starting at the outside and pulling it out the middle. Pull the end taut.

5 Take the other long end and pass it under three of the wraps, starting at the outside and pulling it out the middle. Pull the end taut. When your captive struggles, the loops around the wraps tighten, locking them in place so they can't tighten around the wrist or ankle.

Don't Come Untied: Be careful not to make the wraps too tight to begin with. You don't need to; they are secure even if they are only fairly snug, and if you make them too tight, you will cut off circulation, forcing you to untie your captive long before you want to.

Figure Eight Knot

A nice smooth knot used as an ending for a rope – stopping it from slipping inside a hole or ring or preventing unravelling.

How To Do It: Form a figure-of-eight with the end of the rope, passing the short end through the first loop. Pull to tighten.

Don't Come Untied: Make sure the rope is thick so the knot doesn't just slip through the ring or hole.

Crossed Limbs Binding

Use when you want to tie your partner's hands at the back or front or to tie the ankles with the knees apart.

How To Do It: Rest the centre of the rope against their crossed limbs. Coil the rope around the limbs three or four times. Cross the ends of the rope. The one that will go down passes over the one that will go up. This step is needed to change the direction on the rope without pinching or putting undue pressure on the limbs. Then coil a couple of times up and down, passing the rope between the limbs vertically. Finally, finish the binding by tying both ends of the rope with a Square knot (see page 51).

Don't Come Untied: Check that you can pass at least a finger between the ropes and the skin. If you can't, loosen the binding and next time, don't make the coils so tight.

Parallel Limbs Binding (Two-Column Tie)

Ties the ankles or wrists so that the arms or knees are pulled tightly together.

How To Do It: Lay the centre of the rope across your partner's limbs and coil it three or four times around both limbs. When the coils are finished, cross the ropes, the one going down over the one going up, as above. Secure things with a couple of vertical coils crossways and finish with a Square knot.

Don't Come Untied: It's the horizontal/vertical hatching that gives this tie its strength so don't pull it too tight while coiling. Make sure you can pass the finger test, slipping one finger between the rope and the skin.

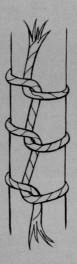

Marling Hitch

Sweet for securing seated poses.

How To Do It: Begin with a Lark's Head (see page 50) around the wrist and the upright of the chair. You will be working from the wrist towards the armpit along the length of the chair's upright. Holding one tail along the length of the arm, wrap the other around the circumference of the arm and chair. When it crosses over the other tail, run the top rope under the bottom rope, forming an overhand knot. Repeat to continue up the arm, making sure that your tension is even, and not too tight. When you reach the underarm, and you cannot make any more knots, tie the end of the rope to the top of the chair back. Repeat on the other side. You can also work this with the doubled length.

Don't Come Untied:
Make sure you cross the top rope over the bottom before going under the bottom. If you don't, you will have Half Hitches rather than overhand knots and it won't hold in place as well.

Bondage Cheat Sheet

Your field guide to the best restraints for your needs.
See page 125 for a cross-reference index to the knots.

If she always wanted to be a Triple Z without the silicone or push up...

Use: The Breast Harness, which is the bondage
version of a push-up bra.

How To Do It:

1 Make a Lark's Head and centre it at her back.

2 Wrap the rope around the front of the body, from left to right,
so that it's pulling against the loop. Continue wrapping the
rope around to the back, under the breasts.

3 Pull the rope through the loop formed when you
wrapped the rope, and begin wrapping in the opposite
direction. When you come around to the back again, pass the rope
through the loop, and reverse direction again.
Continue until you have eight strands of rope.

4 Pass the end of the rope through the loop, and secure it with
a Half Hitch. Pull the ends of the rope taut. Finish off with a Figure
Eight knot at the ends of the rope.

When you want to snag their arms to the banister, porch railing, your office chair...

Use: The French Bowline.

How To Do It: Use the French Bowline cuff to anchor, then tie wrist restraints to the back legs of the chair, just below the seat or railings. Secure in place with a Marling Hitch.

When you are too cheap to spend the dosh on an arm bind...

Use: The Handcuff knot.

How To Do It:

1 Make a bight in the centre of your rope. From the centre, pull out 7.5 cm (3 in) on both sides. Make a loop with one half (loop 1), then make a loop on top of that (loop 2) with the other half (it will look like a Mastercard logo). At the same time, pull the inside of loop 1 forward through loop 2, and pull the inside of loop 2 back through loop 1 to make a double-sided slip-knot.

2 Place each slip-knot over an arm. Slide the loops up to the shoulder like a backpack, then pull on the tails to tighten the loops around the shoulders.

3 Every 10 cm (4 in), along each long tail, create new loops with a chain stitch (wrap the rope around a hand, make an X, push the rope on top, under the rope on the bottom, and tighten the knot).

4 Pull out the loops and slip them over and then up the arms, then pull on the tails to tighten them. Repeat until you get down to the wrist. When doing this, try to keep the arms in the position you want them to be in.

5 Make a Half Hitch or Square knot around the rope ends to finish it off.

If he wants a permanent stiffy...

Use: Adapt the Hair Bondage techniques on pages 98–101, substituting his appendage for her locks.

When you want to completely immobilize them and have your wicked way...

Use: Crab Legs. Great for restricting leg mobility and getting into their treasure chest.

How To Do It: Have them sit and then use a French Bowline on the wrist. Use the tails to tie a Half Hitch to the legs to band them in place.

When you want to completely immobilize them and tease them mercilessly...

Use: Frog Legs.

How To Do It:

1 Fold the heel as far back to the thigh as possible. Place a bight between the folded leg as high on the thigh as possible, and as low to the ankles as possible.

2 Wrap the tails around the thigh and ankle and pull tightly through to make a Lark's Head.

3 Now pull the tails back in the opposite direction around the ankle and thighs, going up towards the waist. Repeat a couple of times to create a band of rope.

4 Take the tails back down to the original Lark's Head and pull tightly through. Make a Half Hitch to finish.

If you want their arms behind them or their ankles crossed together a la a damsel/hero in distress...

Use: A Crossed Limb Binding.

If you want their arms crossed behind them and you're Godzilla...

Use: A Parallel Limb Binding.

How To Do It: Bend one arm behind the back and hold horizontally, then resting the other arm on top and start wrapping. Up the X factor by doubling up and wrapping both at the wrists and the elbow bend.

If you want to make them dangle...

Use: A French Bowline on the wrists and a Buntline Hitch through to loops on a vertical rope (make sure they're low enough to rest their toes on the floor).

Hint: It helps to have them stand on a box or low stool while tying them up and taking them down.

If you want to stop them from running away...

Use: The Hobble.

How To Do It: Start with a Lark's Head doubled up. The loop should be near one of the limbs. Coil both ends of the rope around both limbs, pass inside the Lark's Head loop and coil in the opposite direction. This may also be used on the wrists, fingers or toes.

When you want them lying flat and open to your wickedest whim...

Use: The Spread Eagle.

How To Do It: Have them spread their arms and legs and secure in place with four French Bowline cuffs.

When you want a crotchrope but have only one rope...

Use: The French Bowline.

How To Do It:

1 Begin with a French Bowline on a bight as the waist belt.

2 Then take the lines from the wrists and run them around the outsides of the thighs and back between the legs, up to the wrist-lines again and back down to create a diamond pattern.

3 Bring the lines together in a Square knot and go back between the legs as a crotchrope, which you bring up and tie off at the waist-belt again.

When you want to get them some sexy underwear but don't want to spend a lot of money...

Use: The G-String Tie. It's quick to do and can be worn all night.

How To Do It:

1 Centre the rope and drape it so it goes around the back of the neck and the ends hang down the front.

2 Lead the rope to the back, under the arms, then cross it at mid-back level, and bring the ends around to the front. Have your partner hold their wrists close together behind their back, and tie each wrist with one of the rope ends coming through between their legs.

3 Bring the ropes around to the front and pull taut. This will bring their wrists to their sides. Tie the rope ends together in front with a Square knot. Put the ends together, pull them up, and tie a knot just underneath the breasts.

4 Bring the rope ends around to the back on each side. Wrap them around the arms and under the breasts several times. Bring the rope ends around to the back, and tie them with a Square knot.

When you want them on their hands and knees, unable to move...

Use: A Karada (see page 72) and Frog Tie (see page 74).

If you want to drive his joystick off the road...

Use: The Marling Hitch.

How To Do It:

1 Loop around the base of his penis and balls. Pull the ends of the cord through the loop and pull it snug. The loop should fall about where the balls attach to his bat.

2 Now take the ends and start the Marling Hitch wrap. Pull the cords around the balls snug and wrap the ends around the base, crossing over the wrap as before. Tuck the ends under the wrap, and pull.

3 The Marling Hitches will loop better if the knots run along the top surface of the penis. To make this happen, slide the crossing you just did around to the top, letting in slack as needed.

4 Repeat the wrap and tuck until you run out of tool. You can take the ends of the cords and tie them to your partner's nipple clamps. Or not.

When you want to tie your lover's arms or legs together and tease them mercilessly...

Use: A French Bowline and Crossed or Parallel Limb Bindings.

When you want to increase the tension...

Use: The Prusik, perfect for tightening the rope after binding.

When you want to finish neatly or add some sting to a whip...

Use: Figure Eights.

When you want to hold the pose...

Use: The Hobble.

When you want to throw them over your knee for a good spanking...

Use: Frog Legs, flipped on to the stomach.

When you want to try knocking at their backdoor...

Use: Reverse Spread Eagle – tie as you would for Spread Eagle, but position them face down.

No Knots Need Apply

If you're all thumbs when it comes to tying knots, don't despair. You can still indulge in some restraint play without getting all bound up. These wraps and devices don't include a single tie. For more no-knot ideas, see pages 110–13.

Karada

An easy form of Shibari, this rope harness can be tied in about 15 minutes, and there's not a single knot in it.

1 Start with an extra-long 15 m (50 ft) rope to leave lots of rope for some bells and whistles once you're done. Make a bight so it drapes around the back of the person's neck with the tails draping down the front of the body.

2 Bring the ends of the rope around one another three times – these three twists will become the three diamonds you see in the front of the finished rope harness. Bring the two ends of the rope between your partner's legs, then up and apart on the other side.

3 From this point, each end of the rope will wrap around their hips and then through the lowest twist in front, which is much easier to do than to read about… See? Nothing to it.

4 Don't pull the rope tight; as you continue this process, bringing the ends of the rope around to the front, passing them through the twists, and then bringing them back again, the rope will need to slide to let the diamonds open up in the front. It's okay if the rope is loose at this point; it will become tighter as you work your way up. Repeat two more times.

5 After the last twist, bring the ends of the rope over the shoulder tops or back around beneath their arms so that the rope goes around to the front of their body, through the topmost twist, then back around behind them again. Now bring the ends up underneath the rope where it passes around the neck, and down beneath the rope, wrapping around their back. (Again, easier than it sounds.)

6 You can tie off or tuck in the ends of the rope wherever you like — around the part where it loops around the back of the neck, or around the part where it crosses behind their back — but that would be a waste of a good rope. Instead, segue into a Frog Tie — see page 74.

Frog Tie

1 Tell your partner to kneel. Take the leftover rope and bring it down between your partner's legs. Then pass it under and up around the leg, and keep wrapping around the person's leg a few times so that it is snug but not tight.

2 Bring it between their upper and lower leg, pass it around all the wrappings and back between their upper and lower leg again. At this point, you'll adjust how tight the wrappings are around the leg – the tighter you pull the loop of rope around the wrappings, the tighter they'll be.

3 From there, take the end of the rope up along the person's inner thigh. Almost done – just take whatever amount of rope is left at the end and wrap it around and around the lower part of the Karada where it comes across their bottom. When you've reached the end, just tuck the last bit of rope underneath the wrap.

Chain Harness

You can also make a Karada out of chain. The chain should have openable links because it won't wrap or tie like rope.

1 Start with a 10 m (33 ft) length of chain, find the bight and slip it over your partner's head so that it hangs down the front of their body.

2 Twist the chain and hold the twisted sections open to create diamonds in the front (command your partner to hold the chain or you may lose the diamond).

3 Bring the ends down between their legs, then up behind them, around their body, and through the section in front.

4 Repeat until you reach the top, then bring it over their shoulders and down their back. Use a chain link that can be opened, a small padlock or carabineer to link the chain together behind their neck.

5 Take the excess length of chain and tuck it beneath the chain, passing around the body. You can secure them to a fixed object or leave it hanging like a tail between their legs.

Under-the-Bed Restraints

Skip the complicated hardware. This simple, discreet cuff set, made to stay in place in your bed with a connector slide, renders your lover helpless in a snap. Available from good sex shops (try www.lovehoney.co.uk or www.amazon.com), they are particularly useful for those who have beds without bedposts, as the straps are anchored under the mattress and can be positioned in various ways. They can also be linked together end-to-end and worn as a collar or thigh cuff.

Warning: Bad Ideas

Zip ties hold the tie well but are almost impossible to remove and can cut into flesh, while electrical cord can't hold the knot well, no matter how much of an extra electrical charge it gets. Don't use these!

Bondage for Boobs

To Flatten:
Bondage tape, ace bandages, plastic wraps

To Tease:
Ice cubes, nipple clamps, feathers

To Torture:
Paddle, spanking, nibbling, scratching

To Restrain:
Nipple clamps, tight corset

Chapter Four

Pleasure Bound

When most people think of bondage, they simply think of a person being tied up, possibly smacked around a bit… and that's it. But there's oh-sigh-much more you can do when your sex life is all tied up. Most bondage beginners tend to dive in and start tying, knotting, hitching and splicing as if their life depended on it. But every carnal connection, regardless of its kink level, starts with foreplay. Skipping the warm-up can cut the amount of pleasure you take in a scene.

Build the anticipation with some sexual intercourse – the talking kind. You are going to need to discuss what you plan to do with each other anyway to set the necessary boundaries of how far you're willing to go. But don't make this a formal interview complete with checklists (unless that's part of your fantasy). Send flirty emails and suggestive text messages. Check out pictures in magazines and read books that have bondage themes. Alison Tyler's bondage and erotica series is a good page-turner. Once you're ready to play, ease into the scene with lots of caresses and cuddles and soft touches. This makes it easier and more sensually intense when you work up to fiercer moves.

Once the person playing "bottom" is fit to be tied, the "top" may be tempted to stop all loving touches and become all businesslike as they truss them up – especially if they're a knotting novice. But this is part of the fun – keep stroking, squeezing and snuggling as the binds tighten, gradually increasing the tempo and intensity. The idea is to tease them into a frothy frenzy until they beg for mercy. Here's how…

PART ONE *Tie Me Up*

For bondage beginners, getting started can be the hardest part. So skip the restraints at first. Verbal bondage can be just as kinky, naughty and taboo as physical bondage. Simply commanding your lover or being commanded to do something or lie back and take it can be a pelvis-pumping thrill.

To get things going, dress the part. Yes, you'll get undressed later, but nothing gets you in the mental mood faster than the right outfit. Thigh-high boots, a corset, a naughty teddy, anything leather… whatever makes you feel in control or ready to be controlled.

Once you're in costume, let
the play begin. Stay in role
until the climax.

Beginner's Steps

1 The top starts by telling the bottom to do exactly as they say, and that absolutely no deviation from those commands is permitted. The top then undresses the bottom and has them lie down with arms overhead and eyes closed. They are not to move, squirm, or open their eyes no matter what. The top then explains, in detail, precisely what they intend to do, and how much pleasure it will give them to take possession of the bottom's helpless body.

2 The top can then work in some sensory teases, running their fingernails lightly up and down their victim's body, paying close attention to sensitive areas that normally don't get touched very much, such as the undersides of the arms, thighs, face and neck.

   They should take their time, and be on the watch for any movement from the bottom – the idea is that they are being restrained by sheer force of will. So if they move, the top should sternly tell them that they're breaking the rules, followed by a quick nipple twist or slap to the inner thigh for emphasis.

3 Once you're both up to speed with the dirty talk and sexual commands, ramp up the action with a little actual bondage. Restraining the hands is the best way to begin – it immediately restricts freedom without making the person being tied feel totally helpless. But if you prefer to begin at the bottom with the ankles, go for it.

   The important thing is to keep it just between the two of you. Don't include ties to the bed or a chair or a suspension bar just yet. The

person being bound needs to feel confined, not cemented in place. They want to know that they can escape if they need to (at first, anyway).

4 Once you're comfortable with how things are, you can move on to Spread Eagle or a chair tie (see pages 60 and 67). After that, you've earned your bondage badge and can take your pick of ties, restraints and positions.

The Intermediate Stage

So, now what? What does one actually do with a partner who's at your mercy, bound to the bed?

1 Before you do anything, slip a blindfold on them. Covering the eyes increases the sense of powerlessness and anticipation still more.

2 Then sit. Drive them out of their mind not knowing what's to come – or indeed, whether you're even still on the premises.

3 After a few minutes, quietly slide over and begin with a thorough body massage, with just a hint of kink. Pour some massage oil along your partner's body, or better still, use some body wax candles, which burn cooler than regular candles and turn into massage oil when you pour the hot drippings on to your partner's body. Straddle your partner and give them a very long, sensual massage. Work your way down their body, paying special attention to love buds. Keep going south, lingering over their inner thighs, teasing but not quite touching their hot spots.

4 Now make things a bit more interesting. Slide an ice cube over various places – sides, feet, arms, chest, belly, thighs, hands, in rapid and unpredictable succession, leaving it in contact for longer and longer periods of time. Keep reinforcing the "don't move" order.

5 Talk to them as you play. Tease them with little suggestive comments, or investigate how they're enjoying things. Take requests, if you do such things. Most of all, be sure they know you're having a down and delightfully dirty time. But don't talk incessantly; shut up occasionally and do your job.

6 Just when they're getting numb to your cool touch – and the ice cube has melted to a chip – switch to something with a sharper, more pointed sensation. You can use a bamboo skewer, toothpick, comb or, if you're a gadget person, a Wartenberg wheel – a wheel of prickly little pins that can be rolled over a person's skin.

  The contrast between the ice (which your partner is expecting) and a very different kind of sensation (which your partner isn't) should make them moan (and jump, giving you a chance to indulge in your master and commander role and warn them, with a slap to the sensitive inner thigh, that you did not give them permission to move).

7 Keep mixing up the stimulation in unpredictable ways. Your MVP (Most Valuable Player) here is the senses – all five. Even the most minor of sensory plays – like a quick kiss on the belly – can feel excrucia-tingly good when it is unexpected. See the Extra-Sensory Moves opposite for more ideas.

Ten Extra-Sensory Moves

Here are ten wall-shaking, earth-quaking sensational moves that'll make your partner end up across the room (you might want to tie them down, too).

Use one or all. Think of them as your must-do list of starter techniques to tie, sigh, tease, squeeze and totally please. Be prepared – they'll beg you give them relief (and isn't that the idea?). If you're feeling particularly evil, don't offer any relief at all! But definitely take your turn – when you're ready, straddle (face or groin – you get to choose) and instruct them on exactly how to bring you pleasure.

1 Mute It

Cover their ears with ear muffs, earphones hooked into music (your choice if you make it something they love or hate) – anything that restricts hearing so they can concentrate on how their other senses are being tortured. Up the amps with an OhMiBod music-powered vibrator.

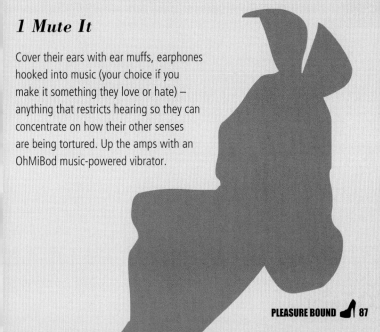

2 Be Breast in Show

When they're all wrapped up with no place to go, you can:

- Add a cold chill to your play by wrapping the breasts in chains that have been stored in the freezer.

- Pinch an inch. Nipples can be some of the most sensitive bits on the human body – his and hers. You can buy nipple clamps, vibroclips and tweezers that adjust to add just the right squeeze, but clothespegs (clothespins) and rubberbands are good emergency subs. Nip tip – the less skin you pinch, the more it will hurt. Don't leave it on for more than 15 minutes at a time. Don't worry that it's not long enough – the really exquisite ache starts when the pressure is released.

- Load up on bondage tape and wrap up the chest to form a tight boob tube.

- Drip warm wax around the exposed flesh of breasts wrapped in a chest harness (see Karada pages 72–73).

- Crank up the heat by alternating with an ice cube rub.

3 Make Surprise Moves

When you're making your way up your partner's body, be it with kisses or with drizzled syrup, going in a straight line doesn't work as effectively as zig-zagging. Nerves like surprises, and if you're working in a straight line, the body knows what's coming next.

4 Use Your Mouth

Bondage without oral should simply be considered wrong. Bondage with straight-through-to-orgasm oral should also be considered wrong. But bondage with teasing, tantalizing oral – oo la la! Kiss and suck and bite them all over, then return again to some straight oral play. Toy with them manually. Change gears as often as you're able.

5 Just Add Water

...Or lube, as the case may be. When liquid combines with bondage, you get awesome surface tension.

6 Add Pain to Pleasure

This isn't about drawing blood (unless you want to). But bondage and spanking or smacking with a whip or paddle go together. As a rule, strokes from whips and paddles are delivered to fleshy, muscled body areas such as the lower buttocks and the "lower half of the upper half" of the back. But you can also use a nylon rope flogger that's been frayed out, a ribbon flogger made of thin strands of satin ribbon or a rubber duster whip made of thin rubber strings about the size of angel-hair pasta, which let you whack away without the pain (no matter how hard you hit).

WARNING: It's very dangerous to strike kidneys, liver, spleen or tailbone.

7 Tickle

Watch them wiggle and squirm. Use your fingers or, better yet, a feather (there are specific ticklers made for the purpose available from sex shops). Run it up the small of the back and below the buttocks for a totally tantalizing sensation.

8 Heat Things Up With Wax

Put your partner in a horizontal position (it makes it much easier
to drip wax onto them). Have some ice cubes handy to cool their skin.
If they're into the pain as well as the pleasure, scrape off the wax
with your fingernails afterwards.

9 Mummify – Safely

Zip into a microfleece sleeping bag together. You'll feel completely
enclosed.

10 Use Household Objects

Your house is chockablock with bondage gear. Try dragging the prongs of
a fresh-from-the-freezer ice-cold fork up the inside of their leg, or teasing
their privates with the bristles of a silicone pastry brush. Use a curtain
tassel to tease and tickle. Even a piece of paper being dragged up a naked
body will make them shiver. A comb or brush, body lotion, a paintbrush:
anything works, provided you begin with light pressure and see what the
reaction is.

Timed and Primed

You don't need to hole up in your bedroom for the weekend to have a bondage blast. These titillating techniques are paced to suit any schedule.

When you only have five minutes

Use a vibrator. Tie your partner spread-eagled to the bed and rest a vibrator between their legs. While they writhe around trying to get the buzz exactly where they want, you can speed things up even more by adding some oral love.

When you have only 15 minutes

For this one, he needs to be the bottom. All you need is a plain scarf. Place it around his meat and two veg, and tie in a large Square knot, leaving about 30 cm (12 in) of fabric on each end to hold on to. As you're riding him, pull on the free ends so that the knot rubs against your clitoris. Constricting his penis and scrotum will lead to a harder erection, which will make you both grin from ear to ear.

When you have 30 minutes

Multitask. First, blindfold your partner. Then hit all their passion points at once. When you suck and bite a nipple, use a hand to tease an inner thigh and the other hand to toy with an ear lobe. Remember, they can't see what's coming. Every touch, every action will cause an incredible mix of feelings. Mix and remix every time you do this.

When you have an hour

You have two choices:

1 Mess with their mind and mislead where you strike next.
Fasten your partner's hands together and blindfold them for a game of Tease 'n' Tie. Since crawling over them on the bed is pretty much a suspense killer, try to work from the side of the bed. If you can, pull your bed out from the wall. Having 360-degree access means you can do more to them and you have more ability to move around. Also try to minimize how often you lean onto the bed, because, again, they can feel the weight shifting, thus destroying the surprise advantage.

Then drag a finger up their chest, trace it over their lips, and when they think they can suck on it, pop a cherry or sweet in their mouth – or your tongue. Slowly lick their chest and nipples, then stop for a few seconds. Next, stroke their love triangle. Stop again. Not knowing what you're going to do next really drives them wild, to the point where they'll be begging you to untie them (if they do, make sure they return the favour – and them some).

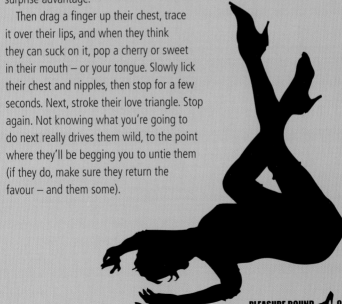

2 Play the numbers.

Once your partner is securely tied and blindfolded, arrange some toys and implements nearby – clothespegs (clothespins) or clamps, a vibrator, a paddle or crop, an ice cube, whatever else strikes your fancy. Assign a number between one and however many of the various items you have to each one. Then have your partner in crime pick a number and a part of the body, such as "seven left nipple", "four inner thigh", or whatever. Use that implement on that part of the body – clamp a clothespeg to your partner's left nipple, run the ice cube along his or her thigh, and so forth. If you have time, randomly scramble the numbers, and do it again.

When you have two hours

Again, he needs to be the bottom. Tie him to a chair and do a striptease followed by a lap dance. Grind your groin against his while rubbing baby oil into your breasts. Lean forward every now and then and let them hang in his face, just out of tongue reach.

When you have a few hours

Role-play. Choose naughty student and teacher, cop and naughty convict, or whatever your favourite bondage fantasy is. Costumes optional.

When you have all night

Restrain them, stimulate them but don't let them come to the party fully until you give the OK sign. You can increase his restraints by securing him in a cock ring, which will also give him all-night-long staying power (though they should not be worn for more than 30 minutes at a stretch). You'll need to know what your partner's point of no return is so that you can stop all stimulation when they get too close to the edge. When you do give permission, hold on – the results will be explosive.

Sushi for Two

Combine dinner with your bondage play.
Fresh from Japan (where else?) comes *nyotaimori*,
or the ritual of eating sushi off the body of a naked
person (it's usually a woman but you can take turns).
The arrangement of the sushi on the naked person is
pretty straightforward (though you might want to keep the
wasabi and soy sauce in a separate container). Arrange the
sushi on your partner's body in any way you find aesthetically
pleasing. It should be cold to increase the sensation. They
need to stay very, very still to keep the sushi from falling off.

Traditionally, the rules of *nyotaimori* forbid addressing or
touching the person upon whose body the sushi is served,
but traditions are made to be broken, so touch, caress
and whisper sweet commands to your heart's desire.
Run the ends of the chopsticks lightly over sensitive
parts of your partner's body or use to pinch
their nipples. Warm up some sake and rest
the cup against their skin (make sure it
isn't hot enough to burn them).

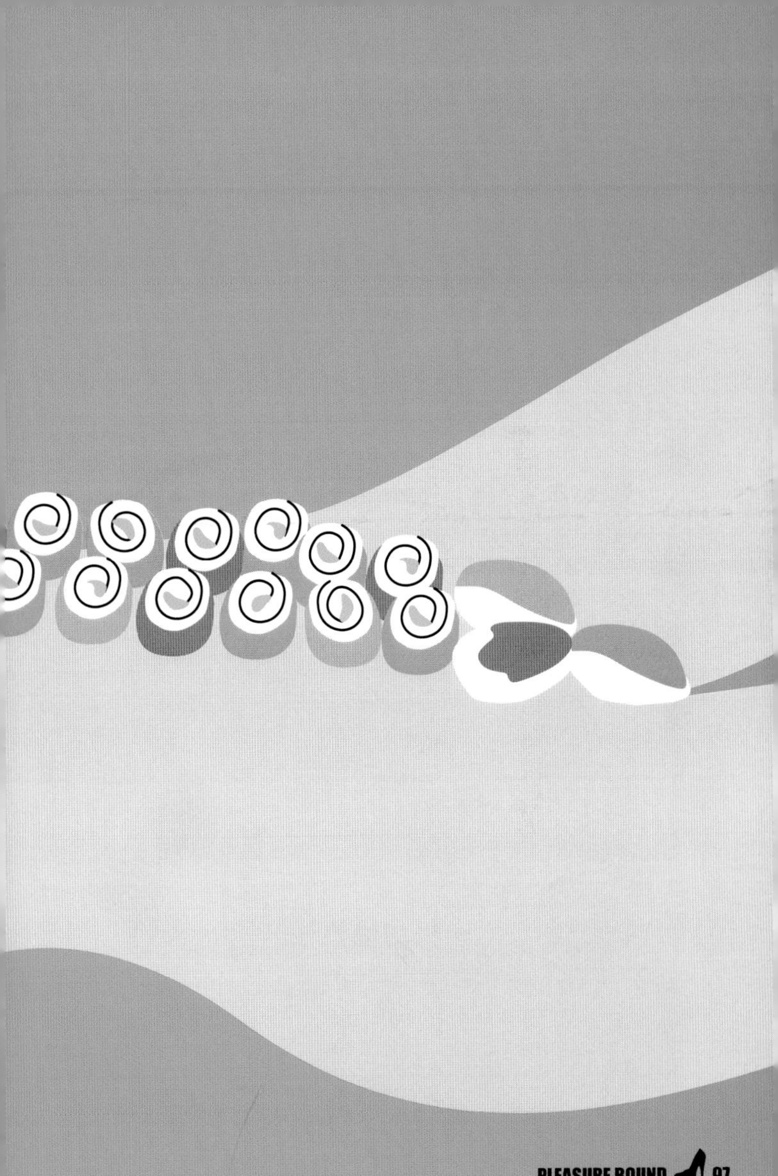

PART TWO *Tie Me Down*

These are six very advanced techniques for broken-in bondage players – only for those of you who are a bit more advanced with putting on the restraints and are looking for new thrills.

1 Hair Bondage

While you don't need to be a trained stylist, you should feel comfortable tying knots – working your tresses into your power play can be fussy as it is easy to brush up against accidental scalping if you tie too tight. Apart from the feeling it gives of being restrained, it also makes for handy control to keep the head still and in position for "forced" oral sex.

Skip the headache if you have short hair. It won't work. But if your locks are shoulder-length or longer, gather the hair in a loose ponytail at the back centre of the head and give it a spritz of hairspray. This will make the hair less slippery so it will stick to the rope and to itself.

This is one time you want to make your knots and pulls as tight as possible.

The Ring

This may work on slightly shorter hair (you'll need a high frustration threshold) and it's a good beginner tie. Take a strand of hair, lead it through a ring (any kind of ring will do, such as those found in hardware and DIY shops) and fold it around it. Make sure the part between the head and the ring is one-third of the hair and the part that's folded back is two-thirds. Wrap either thin packing rope or fishing line around the folded strand, starting from the ring and working towards the head. When finished, fold the remaining one-third upwards and repeat the wrapping, this time up towards the ring. Tie the rope with a Square knot (see page 51). Now the ring can be used as a connection point for any other bondage (the possibilities are endless: from tying the bottom's hands behind their head to fastening the ring to a wall hook or a quick snap-hook to link it to handcuffs).

Japanese Braiding

Japanese bondage masters prefer special rice rope for this, but hemp's rough surface will do just as well. You'll need time to work this intricate method, but the good news is that once tied correctly, it can be kept in for days and used for a wide variety of moves. Take three or four thin ropes and bunch them together as one rope. Lay the middle of the bundle behind the ponytail and wrap both ends around the tail two or three times, about one third of the length of the ponytail from the head. Next divide both the rope bundle and the hair into three strands and plait (braid) them again, going down as far as you can. When done, separate the rope from the hair and tie the rope strings together with a series of Square knots (see page 51). You can now either use the remainder of the rope bundle (if long enough) to tie it to something else or tie another rope to the end of the braided bundle to use in the rest of your bondage.

The Knot Tube

Again, break out the hemp rope. Separate a strand of hair (or use an entire ponytail) and work from the middle of the rope. Wrap it around the strand close to the head once and make a Square knot (see page 51), stopping halfway. Now lay the strand of hair over the knot and make another half reef knot. Wrap the rope around the strand again and repeat the procedure. Repeat this over and over again.

2 Use a Pretzel Hogtie

This is the most strenuous restraint you can do without actually tying someone down. Gag and/or blindfold your bottom. The wrists are hogtied back tightly to the ankles or knee ropes. A shoulder harness is then secured to the ankle ropes and pulled until the spine bends back. Then the big toes are tied together, and the gag or the blindfold is leashed back to the big toes and pulled until the head and neck are arched back. Schedule a trip to the physical therapist.

3 Get Suspended

Almost any suspension is going to cause at least medium discomfort. Put a short (as in 15 minutes max) time limit or use a full-support suspension such as a swing, sling or thigh-straps to support the weight of the body to avoid the suspension damaging your body. Tie the wrists and ankles where and how you desire. You'll need some sort of suspension bar to hang from. And definitely invest in a panic snap, which is designed to be able to be opened even under high tension by sliding a spring-loaded metal collar upward.

4 Pretend to Rape Her

According to studies, being forced into sex is the most common female fantasy. It can be as simple as jumping on your partner by surprise when she comes home from work, wrestling her to the ground, and having your way with her. If anonymity is the turn-on, he can wear a hood – a ski mask, hoody or tights (pantyhose) work just as well. Have some cuffs set up in advance; nothing kills the scene quicker than fumbling around for rope while your "victim" is waiting (im)patiently.

5 Play Hide the Sausage

You know you want to. Anal exploration is one of those teetering-on-the-edge acts – you may be curious about it and want to try it, but you need that extra – shall we say – prod? Being tied up means you can pretend that you have no say in where your partner decides to stick things, whether it be their fingers, fist, hand, tongue, rod, a vibrator or even a butt plug. One caveat – anal sex is not supposed to hurt. So make sure you have plenty of just-in-case lube on hand – apply and reapply.

6 Get Some Kinbaku Under Your Belt

These involve a lot of patience and just as much practice. You will learn how to wrap lengths of rope in specific patterns around certain parts of the body, and eventually the body as a whole, with varying degrees of pressure and constriction, depending on which part of the body is being targeted and stimulated. The rope is usually made of hemp or jute, but silk ropes are just as effective and friction-free for a smoother experience. They'll need to be around 7 m (23 ft) long. The two most well-known patterns are the Ushiro Takatekote and the Ebi.

Ushiro Takatekote (aka Arm Box Tie)

This forms the basis of the majority of Shibari ties and provides a foundation for encompassing the whole body. You will need a rope about 10 m (33 ft) long.

1 Begin by positioning the arms folded behind the back, hands to elbows. Fold the rope in half to create a bight (see page 50).

2 Wrap the wrists together three times, leaving a little slack.

3 Finish the wrists by passing the tails of the rope under all the bands around the wrists and tie off with a Square knot (see page 51), two Half Hitches (see page 52), or even a slipknot if you want the possibility of quick release (but who would after you put in all of that hard work?). The wrists are tied separately from the main chest harness so that they can be released if the arms need to be repositioned.

4 Now take the rope ends and wrap them around the upper body –
around the outside of the arms above the breasts. Wrap all the way
to the back and loop under the rope coming up from the wrists. Now
wrap your rope back in the opposite direction but below the breasts,
continuing around the upper body again to the centre position at the
back and looping under the centre rope. Wrap around one more time in
the opposite direction below the breasts and tie off at the back.

5 For some finishing flourishes, add a *sakuranbo* or crotch rope harness.
Using three thin ropes of about 2 m (6 ft) in length, fold the first rope in
half and wrap it loosely around the waist; pull the two ends through the
bight just below the navel. Run the rope between the thighs, then over
the bottom cheeks and up to the loop around the waist. Use a Square
knot (see page 51) to tie the two ends to the waist rope on either side
of the spine (never on the person's spine).

   If you want to make it more stimulating you can tie knots where the
rope crosses the clit and the bum. Wrap the remaining ropes around the
thighs several times and fix them on the outer sides. The loose ends of
each rope (about 30–40 cm/12–15 in) are run from the outer side of
the thighs up to the waist rope and fixed to it beside the spine.

Ebi (aka Shrimp)

Originally a torture tie, this is one of the most efficient ways to bond with your partner (literally and figuratively) and open them up for any kind of play. Start with a Karada, or chest harness (see pages 72–73).

1 Fold the arms across the front of the chest with the fingertips of each hand touching the elbow of the opposite arm. Tie the arms together with a Parallel Limbs Binding (see page 59). Secure the wrists to the chest harness.

2 As your partner sits on the floor, tie their crossed ankles with whatever knot you want. This forces their shins to be at right angles to each other with the knees wide apart.

3 The ends of the ankle rope are pulled up to and tucked into the chest harness, forcing the legs up. Then pull the ends until the ankles touch the chest. Tie off with a Square knot (see page 51).

4 If there is any free rope, it may be run round the back of the tied person's neck and tied off. Alternatively, the loose end may be wrapped round other ropes and tied off, using whatever knot you like.

Coming Back to Earth

You've tied, you've sighed, now what? After the scene winds down, you still need to unwind things. Limbs that have been wrapped up need a few minutes to recover. Have something warm handy to put over your partner's body – removing ties almost invariably lowers body temperature as the circulation has been somewhat restricted. Really sweet "tops" (and those who want to be able to be on top again) will give their "bottom" a soothing massage.

PART THREE *Self Help*

You don't necessarily need a partner in crime to practise self-bondage. But any all-by-myself play should definitely be embarked upon with caution. AEFs or Autoerotic Fatalities (yes, they are so common there is even a name for it) are unintentional deaths caused by solo sexual gratification activities.

Most AEFs are the result of asphyxiation from nooses or gags gone wrong. But many are also due to complications arising from physical restraint getting all knotted up. Experienced bondage players recommend that if a person decides to engage in self-bondage in spite of the risks, they should prepare a current legal will, in case of accidental death.

Seven Self-Restraints

Here are seven restraints you can do fairly safely on your own. With most of these stimulation bondage techniques, you can be tied up while you go to work, shopping or out with your friends, with no one suspecting a thing (although the goofy grin on your face may be a dead giveaway).

1 Wear a corset.

2 Pinch on a nipple clamp.

3 Slip into a Karada (see pages 72–73).

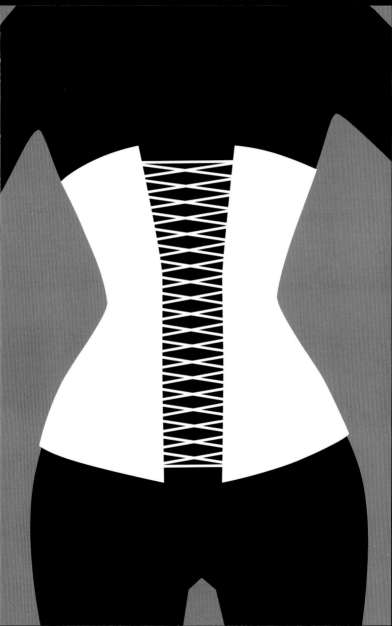

4 Tie on a crotch rope (he can wear one too). The key is to tie the rope so that it stays centred over your best bits. Nylon braided rope is best. If you use cotton rope, put it on over nylon or silk panties otherwise the rope will rub the skin the wrong way – and you'll get so sore you won't want to have sex for at least a week.

- Fold a 9 m (30 ft) rope into a bight and loop around your waist.

- Make a knot on the front.

- Pass the rope ends down between your legs, up to your sides to the front, and under the waist rope.

- Pass it once more between your legs to the back, but around each corresponding leg (just under your bottom) and to the front.

- Pass the ends under the rope on the front, pull and tie a knot on each side.

For an intense extra buzz, secure a vibrator against your love triangle. Don't plan to leave the house – or at least, don't plan on being able to walk.

5 Do it in plain sight with hair bondage (see pages 98–101).

6 Use a timed lock release, available from bondage shops (see page 127). You can restrain yourself and be very sure that you won't be able to get away for at least 1$\frac{1}{2}$ hours! Your bonds will open all by themselves. Enough time to have a few happy moments.

7 Stay glued to your chair. Sitting, secure your left foot with a Velcro cuff (for easy and quick release) around the left chair leg. If you can, also fasten your thigh or at least your knee to the chair. Do the same for the other side. Your legs should now be tied up to the chair. Add some nipple clamps and a vibrator and you may never get up.

Bondage Directory

GLOSSARY OF TERMS

24/7: Total power-exchange relationship.

Abrasion: Any form of sensation play involving stroking or brushing the skin with rough, textured objects such as sandpaper, emery boards and the like. Ouch.

Armbinder (aka single or mono glove): A restraint device consisting of a long sleeve into which both arms are placed, often fitted with laces or straps to hold the arms securely together. May also be used for extreme diets.

Asymmetric Bondage: Not the handiwork of someone who is all thumbs when it comes to making knots. Rather, this refers to any tied-up situation in which a person is purposely bound in an unevenly arranged position, with one leg extended and the other bent, for example. Many forms of Shibari include asymmetric bondage.

Auto-Erotic Asphyxia: A specific form of breath control in which a person when flying solo constricts their own breathing, often with a rope or similar implement, while masturbating. This is really not a good idea – as the estimated 1,000 deaths in the USA per year due to this practice confirms.

Ball-Busting: He may think it's his girlfriend, but the term really applies to any form of genitorture applied to the testicles, as by squeezing, impact or binding.

Ball Gag: A gag – not the April Fool's kind – consisting of a ball, usually made of rubber, which is attached to a strap. The ball is placed in the mouth and the strap is placed around the head to hold it securely in place.

Ball Tie: A specific form of bondage in which the person is bound in a seated position with the knees up, the head bent down over the knees, and the hands behind the back. This posture is for the strong of heart only as it quickly becomes extremely fatiguing.

Bandage Scissors: Specialized scissors, often used by emergency medical personnel, consisting of a pair of scissors with one sharp blade and one blunt blade with a rounded end. The blunt blade can be slid beneath bandages or anything else wrapped tightly around a limb without risk of cutting or injuring the person. Brilliant!

BDSM: A triple decker sandwich. B&D = bondage and discipline; D&S = dominance and submission; and S&M = sadomasochism. Hold the mayo.

Bend: A knot that binds the ends of two ropes together. Also what you need to do if you want to incorporate a little S&M-lite into your play.

Berkley Horse: A type of suspension bondage furniture consisting of a padded bench with restraints and a pair of "arms" to which a person's legs can be affixed.

Bight: A rope folded back on itself to form a narrow loop. Dentists recommend that you never bite your bight.

Binding: A knot that restricts object(s) by making multiple winds. Also, what too many hamburgers will do to your system.

Body Bag: A long, heavy bag, often shaped like a narrow sleeping bag and typically made of canvas, rubber or latex, used to restrain a person very tightly. Sometimes includes integrated straps that wrap around the person within the bag.

Body Harness: A harness consisting of a series of straps designed to be worn around the torso, which may optionally include a mechanism for locking the harness into place and may also include rings or other attachments for ropes, cuffs or chastity belts. Neigh!

Bondage Belt: A belt used to restrain a person, which consists of a heavy band of leather or a similar material that can be strapped or locked about the waist and which has several attachment points to which the subject's wrists may be bound. For those who are all thumbs.

Bondage Bunny: Someone who likes being tied or bound. No tail required.

Bondage Mitt/ Mitten: A fingerless mitten, often made of leather, canvas, heavy vinyl, PVC or similar materials, which is placed over the hand and then fastened in place with an integrated buckling or locking cuff. The bondage mitt holds the hand flat or balled up, and prevents the wearer from being able to pick things up or otherwise make use of his or her hands. So don't expect any frisky finger moves.

Bondage Tape: A vinyl tape material, available in many colours, which sticks only to itself but not to other materials such as skin or clothing, making it ideal for bondage – and Christmas gift-wrapping. Use it to bond, blindfold, gag and restrain. It's easy to remove and unlike regular tape, won't hurt.

Bottom: The submissive in power sex.

Box Tie: A specific form of bondage in which a person brings their arms together, grips each forearm with the opposite hand, and then ropes are wound around them. Talk about being tightly wound!

Breaking Strength: The manufacturer's estimation of the load a rope (on new rope without knots or kinks) will bear before it ruptures. May also be your partner's level of patience when you promise for the fiftieth time to coil the ropes after play.

Breast Bondage: A specific form of bondage involving binding around or over her bubbas.

Breast Press (Breast Clamp): A type of device, often consisting of two horizontal wooden planks with an adjustable screw or clamp mechanism between them, which can be clamped over the breasts – turning her into a mammary sandwich.

Breath Control: Any practice in which a person's breathing is constricted or interrupted, as with a hand or ligature around the throat or with a covering over the face, for the purpose of increasing sexual arousal or sexual climax. Potentially dangerous and can lead to permanent injury or death. Not exactly the orgasmic result you were looking for.

Bullwhip: A type of single tail consisting of a woven or braided leather whip, usually longer than 1.2 m (4 ft) and sometimes 1.8 m (6 ft) long or more, with a short rigid handle. You'll need to be a real cowhand to handle this baby properly. Yeehaw.

Butt Plug: A sex toy designed for anal penetration that has a flared base. Usually smaller than a typical dildo and not shaped like a penis, it is used to give the wearer a very "full" feeling.

Butterfly Chair: A chair that contains two horizontal planks to which the legs can be secured. It is affixed to a pivot so that the legs of the secured person can be spread apart. Otherwise known as a visit to the gynaecologist.

Cable Loop/Slapper: A tool used for striking, consisting of a loop or occasionally two loops of thick wire, coated with plastic, rubber or leather, and affixed to a handle. A cable loop can be used much like a crop or similar implement, and produces intense sensations and really good reception.

Cable Tie/Cuff: A type of cuff consisting of a thin plastic strip with a row of teeth in its surface, and a small ratchet on one end. The end of the cable tie can be placed through the ratchet to form a loop, which can be pulled tight but not loosened again. Sometimes used by police instead of handcuffs. Remember to have scissors handy.

Capsize: A knot that distorts while under strain. May also be what happens to your dining-room chair when you try and turn it into a love hammock.

Cat: Not your household pet or the new orgasmic version of missionary. Instead, this is slang for a cat-o'-nine tails, a specific type of flogger consisting of a handle, often made of wood and wrapped with cloth, with nine lashes affixed to it. The lashes, usually made of rope or of leather, are braided or knotted.

Chastity Belt: Any device intended to prohibit contact with or stimulation of the genitals. Female chastity belts often take the form of a lockable harness that passes between the legs and around the waist; male chastity belts may include a locking enclosure into which the penis is placed. You know he isn't a cheating liar when he slips into one of these.

CHDW: Colloquial term for Clueless Horny Dom Wannabe.

Cock and Ball Torture (CBT): Any way that involves pain play of the penis and testicles – groin kicks during a footie match not included.

Cock Bondage: Tying or restraining the penis. Or marriage for some men.

Cock Ring: A ring (often made of metal or rubber) or strap that's designed to be affixed around the base of an erect penis. The ring allows blood to flow into the penis but constricts the penis sufficiently to prevent blood from flowing out, preventing the penis from becoming flaccid once it is erect. Now she can lead him around.

Coil: Rope looped into a series of neat circles for storage. This is good. What you want to avoid is "recoil". This is bad.

Collar: An item worn around the neck, sometimes equipped with a locking device to prevent its removal, and often worn as a symbol of submission. A diamond necklace will do nicely.

Cordage: A general term to cover all sorts and sizes of rope. After you use them, he should give her a corsage.

Corset: An article of clothing, often made of leather, PVC or vinyl and sometimes including strips of rigid "boning", which is tightly laced and designed to narrow the waist and lift the breasts, creating an hourglass figure.

Coxcombing: A continuous set of hitches of one or more strands to cover a part of the body. Can you say "Coxcombing the coxcomb" ten times fast?

Crop: Also called a riding crop, this is a thin, flexible instrument used for striking, consisting of a sturdy but flexible shaft wrapped with leather or a similar material, with a handle at one end and often with a small leather loop at the other.

Crossing Turn: A circle of rope made with the rope crossing itself. This has nothing to do with changing your mind mid-tie.

Cuff: Any banded restraint, which may be made of metal or of a flexible material such as canvas or leather, for restricting ankles and/or wrists. Don't forget to frisk.

Decorative Knot: A complex knot exhibiting repeating patterns often constructed around and enhancing a part of the body. Also a useful skill for present wrapping.

Eye: The hole inside a circle of rope or a permanent loop made at the end of a rope. Aye-aye!

Fisting: The practice of inserting the entire hand into the vagina or up the bottom. You may need to shake and make up afterwards.

Flogger: A tool with multiple lashes used to strike a person. Also a disciplinarian who administers flogging. Basic but effective.

Forced Orgasm: An orgasm induced in a person against that person's will or as part of resistance play, often by means of bondage combined with sexual stimulation. Sounds good.

Frapping Turns: Additional turns made at right angles in lashings, whippings and seizings to tighten the main turns. Also the way someone dances after too many beers.

Frog Tie: A specific form of bondage in which the person kneels and the ankles are bound to the thighs, preventing the person from rising; the wrists are then bound to the ankles. Kiss and you may turn your frog into a prince(ss).

Gag: Anything used over the mouth to prevent the person from speaking, making loud sounds, or sometimes to hold the mouth open.

Genitorture: Pain play inflicted on the genitals – such as by clamping, pinching, temperature changes or flogging. The operative word is "play".

Grommet: A continuous circle of rope. Also known as a sling. If you want to really mess with their minds, challenge your lover to find the beginning.

Hair Tie/Bondage: Any bondage technique in which a rope, twine or cord is woven or plaited (braided) through a person's hair, then tied in such a way as to limit mobility of the bound person's head.

Half Hitch: A crossing turn, often made round a part of the body or an object. The crossing holds the lower part in place.

Hard Limit: A limit that's considered to be absolute, inflexible and non-negotiable. And that's about as far as they will go.

Hitch: A knot that fastens a rope to part of the body or an object.

Hobble Skirt: A very tight skirt that ends below the knee, which prevents freedom of motion of the legs, allowing the wearer to walk slowly in a hobbling motion. Not something you will see on the catwalk next season.

Hog Slapper: A strap of thick, heavy rubber, often wrapped in burlap or some other coarse material, for slapping when an open palm just won't do.

Hogtie: When the ankles and wrists are bound together, usually behind the back; then the ankles are tied to the wrists while the person lies on his or her stomach. Put on a spit and slowly roast, marinating every 15 minutes.

Hojo Jitsu: A martial art for tying and restraining prisoners.

Hood: Any covering designed to go over the head, often partly or completely covering the face as well. Perfect for avoiding the paparazzi.

Horse: A plank supported by two legs on each end, similar to a sawhorse, for bending over and getting flogged or spanked – or practising one's trots.

Impact Play: Anything involving striking or hitting – for example flogging, spanking, percussion or whipping.

Inversion Table: A flat table to which a person can be bound, and suspended between upright supports on a pivot; the table can be rotated upright, inclined, or turned completely upside-down.

Jam: When a knot cannot be untied readily. In other words, you have a hitch.

Kami: Any technique or tie that involves the hair, such as by weaving ropes through the hair to hold the head immobile.

Karabiner: It sounds like a type of gun but it's actually an oval or D-shaped snap link, usually with a screw lock, used by climbers and industrial riggers.

Karada: A rope harness, originating in Japan, which is tied around the torso in a series of diamond-shaped patterns. Often used as a foundation in Shibari, the Karada does not restrain the subject, and can even be worn under clothing – though perhaps it may just be easier to slip into some lingerie.

Kinbaku: Artistic bondage for expressing your creative inner self.

Kink: A tight turn in a rope that can form during use and may damage rope fibres. Also how bondage is often described.

Knot: The generic word for all rope and cordage tucks and ties.

Kotori: A rope harness intended to support a person's weight from the torso and upper legs. Chopsticks not included.

Laid Rope: Rope made by twisting. And it's very happy.

Lashing: A knot usually used to hold poles together. But may also be what your lover wants to give you.

Lay: The direction of the twist in the rope away from the viewer, either clockwise (right-handed, Z laid) or anticlockwise (left-handed, S laid).

Line: Another word for rope, but generally small cordage of less than 12.5 mm (¹/₂ in) in diameter. Might also be something handed to you in order to get you in a compromising position.

Loop: A knot used to create a closed circle in a line.

Mastigothyma: The official psychological term for getting off on getting flogged. Those who have it just say, "Owww-ohhhhh!"

Mouth Bit: Any of a style of gags with a long cylinder-shaped bit, usually made of soft rubber or latex, in place of a round ball. Mouth bits may include an integrated harness. Ride 'em, cowboy!

Mummification: A form of bondage in which a person is immobilized by being entirely wrapped quite tightly, with plastic wrap, rope, fabric or similar material. Not for the claustrophobic.

Natural Fibre: Processed plant products used to make rope and other cordage. Can include cotton, flax, hemp, jute, manilla, sisal and silk. Good for eco-minded bondage players.

Nipple Clamp: Any device that's designed to be clamped to the nipples. May include a mechanism for adjusting or limiting the amount of pressure applied to the nipple. Clothespegs (clothespins) make good (and cheap!) nipple clamps.

One-Column Tie: In bondage, any form of tie that binds one part of the body to something else – such as the arm to the headboard.

Orgasm Control/Denial: The only way they can come to the party is if they ask. Aka bad lover.

Over the Knee (OTK): A style of spanking which is pretty much what it sounds like. Bottom's up.

Paddle: Any stiff, hard implement, often made of wood, used for striking a person, most commonly on the rear. You never want to go up a creek without one.

Pain Play: Any activity in which one person inflicts pain on a consenting partner for pleasure (eating the last chocolate chip cookie doesn't count).

Percussion: Any form of impact play involving striking with a blunt or fairly heavy implement – such as a buck hammer or bass drum.

Predicament Bondage: A type of bondage in which the intent is to place the bound person in an awkward, difficult, inconvenient or uncomfortable situation, or to set out a challenge for the bound person to overcome. For example, a person might be bound in such a way that their hands and feet are mostly but not completely immobilized, then asked to perform a task (such as to serve their lover a drink or make dinner).

Psychological Bondage: Bondage without the use of ropes or other restraints. It's all in the voice command.

Rope Cuff: Any form of tie that binds the wrists or ankles together. A knowledge of knots is a must.

Rope Splice: A knot formed by interweaving strands of rope rather than whole lines. More time consuming to do, but usually stronger than simple knots and you don't need a ring.

Round Turn: When a rope is wrapped so that it passes around the back of a body part or object twice. If you can follow that, you will have no trouble making strong rope splices.

Running End: Also called the "working end", refers to the tip of the rope that forms a knot, and not what you do once you have trussed up your lover.

Safe Word: A pre-agreed phrase or way to say, "Stop what you are doing now." In other words, no really does mean no.

Seize: To join two ropes or parts of ropes together with a binding of small cordage. May also refer to what you will want to do to your partner if they lose the key to the handcuffs.

Self-Bondage: Tying one's self up or otherwise restraining one's self, sometimes as a part of masturbation. Often tricky and always lonely.

Sensation Play: Any BDSM activity involving creating unusual sensations on a person who may be blindfolded, usually using ice cubes, soft fur or cloth, coarse materials, etc. Feeding spoonfuls of ice cream counts.

Sensory Deprivation: Reducing a person's ability to see, hear or use their senses, creating a heightened state of arousal (read fear).

Shibari: A type of bondage originating in Japan and characterized by extremely elaborate and intricate patterns of rope, often used both to restrain and to stimulate by binding or compressing the breasts and/or genitals. Think of it as two for one.

Shinju: A type of Japanese rope harness that goes around and over the breasts. A shinju does not restrict motion and can be worn under clothing; as the subject moves, the ropes shift against the breasts, providing constant stimulation. Aramaa!

Slapper: Two thick leather paddles bound together at the handle so that when a person is struck, the two paddles hit one another, creating a loud sound. No connection with getting slap happy.

Sling: Leather, canvas or nylon webbing furniture, suspended by chains or cables from the ceiling, for sit-and-swing sex.

Slipknot: A knot tied with a hitch around one of its parts so that you can slide it and adjust the size of the loop, in contrast with a loop, which is closed with a bend. A slipknot can be closed; a loop remains the same size.

Snug: To take the slack out of a knot and tighten it. Sounds cosy.

Spanking Glove: A glove, often made of leather or heavy rubber and frequently (though not always) fingerless, designed to protect the wearer's palm as the wearer spanks another person. The bottom is up for grabs.

Spread Eagle: When a person is lying flat and bound or restrained with legs spread apart and hands over their head. Not for first dates.

Spreader Bar: A rigid bar or rod, often with attachment points for restraints built into it at each end, designed to be attached to the feet or ankles to hold the legs spread apart. May be adjustable in length and may not be used in place of a knee press at the gym.

Sukaranbo/ Sukuranbo: A type of rope harness that wraps around the buttocks and upper thighs and passes between the legs and over the genitals, passing between the lower lips of a female wearer. The rope may feature a knot at the place where it touches the clitoris.

Suspension: Any form of bondage in which the person bound is hanging partially or completely off the floor, often by ropes affixed to an overhead point or by means of a rigid bar with attached suspension cuffs. For serious bondage players only.

Takatekote: A type of rope harness, originating in Japan, which goes around the torso and holds the arms behind the back.

Tweezer Clamps: Long, thin, tweezer-like clamps made of flexible spring steel, with a ring that can be used to adjust their tightness. Among the mildest of all forms of nipple clamp, typically causing little or no pain.

Two-Column Tie: Like the single except two parts of the body are tied together.

INDEX OF KNOTS

Bar Wrap	54
Bight	50
Buntline Hitch	55
Cross Limb Binding	59
Figure Eight	58
French Bowline	55
Frog Tie	74
Half Hitch	52
Karada	72
Lark's Head	50
Marling Hitch	60
Parallel Limb Binding	59
Prusik	56
Shibari Ties	53
Square	51

BONDAGE GEAR, INFORMATION AND TOYS

Ann Summers
For sex toys, costumes, kits and erotica
www.annsummers.com

Babeland
Babe-friendly sex and bondage toys
www.babeland.com

B E S T Slave Training
How-tos for bondage knots and hitches
www.bestslavetraining.com/Bondageknot.htm

Blowfish
Bondage tips and pointers, handbooks and gear
www.blowfish.com/catalog/guides/

Bondage Gear
Hoods, whips, gags, rope and restraints, delivered in discreet packaging
www.bondagegear.co.uk

Coco de Mer
Luxury top-quality bondage gear, such as silver cuffs and collars, leather reins and harnesses, corsets, masks and rope
www.coco-de-mer.com/shop/bondage

Deviants Dictionary
An online guide to bondage terms and knots
public.diversity.org.uk/deviant/ssknots.htm

Extreme Restraints
Quality bondage and fetish gear including furniture, suspension equipment and sleepsacks
www.extremerestraints.com

Good Vibrations
An online sex superstore providing all kinds of bondage and fetish toys, harnesses and strap-ons
www.goodvibrations.com

Lavender's Latex Lair
Latex apparel and accessories for all kinky needs
www.l8tex.com

Libida
Offers harnesses, restraints and other toys, as well as erotica
www.libida.com

Love Honey
Vibrators, gifts, whips and more: the online orgasm superstore
www.lovehoney.co.uk

OhMiBod
Hi-tech sex toys that connect to mobile phones and other sockets
www.ohmibod.com

Ooh La La
Spicy sex toys for girls and boys
www.ooh-lala.co.uk

The Pleasure Chest
A treasure trove of pleasure devices
with a BDSM section
www.thepleasurechest.com

Sexual Health Info Centre
A site providing sexual health advice
as well as a wide range of dildos
www.sexhealth.org

Simply Pleasure
A climactic collection of tools,
including whips, bondage and fetish
www.simplypleasure.com

Stockroom
Quality sex toys, bondage gear,
restraints, chastity belts and more.
www.stockroom.com

Temptations
Tantalizing sex toy supplier which
sells a large BDSM selection, such as
spreader bars, rope and restraints,
fetish furniture, cock and ball toys,
medical sex toys and much more
www.temptationsdirect.co.uk

Tabooboo
Fun site selling costumes, spankers,
leather accessories, restraints and
bondage tape
www.tabooboo.com

FURTHER READING

Bondage for Sex, Chanta Rose,
BDSM Press, 2006

*Consensual Sadomasochism: How
to Talk About It and How to Do It
Safely*, William Henkin and Sybil
Holiday, Daedalus Publishing, 1996

Erotic Bondage Handbook, Jay
Wiseman, Greenery Press, 2000

*The Master's Manual: A Handbook
of Erotic Dominance*, Jack Rinella,
Daedalus Publishing, 1994

*The Mistress Manual: The Good Girl's
Guide to Female Dominance*, Mistress
Lorelei, Greeenery Press, 2000

The New Bottoming Book, Dossie
Easton and Janet W Hardy,
Greenery Press, 2001

The New Topping Book, Dossie
Easton and Janet W Hardy,
Greenery Press, 2001

*The Seductive Art of Japanese
Bondage*, Midori, Greenery Press,
2002

*Shibari You Can Use: Japanese
Rope Bondage and Erotic Macramé*,
Lee "Bridgett" Harrington, Mystic
Productions, 2007